RAINBOWS ARE MADE

RAINBOWS ARE MADE

POEMS BY

CARL SANDBURG

Selected by

LEE BENNETT HOPKINS

Wood engravings by

FRITZ EICHENBERG

HARCOURT BRACE JOVANOVICH, PUBLISHERS

San Diego   New York   London

LIBRARY OF CONGRESS CATALOGING IN PUBLICATION DATA
Sandburg, Carl, 1878–1967.   Rainbows are made.
Includes index.
SUMMARY: Seventy humorous and serious poems dealing with people,
word play, everyday things, nature, night, and the sea.
1. Children's poetry, American.   [1. American poetry]
I. Hopkins, Lee Bennett.   II. Eichenberg, Fritz, 1901–   ill.
III. Title.
PS3537.A618A6   1982   811'.52   82-47934
ISBN 0-15-265480-1

B C D E
First edition

To

ANNA BIER
MARIA MODUGNO
PETER JOVANOVICH

who paved the rainbow

&

to

CARL SANDBURG
for the pot of gold

—LBH

CONTENTS

"Poetry is a search for syllables to shoot at the barriers of the unknown and the unknowable."

"Poetry is a shuffling of boxes of illusions buckled with a strap of facts."

"Poetry is a phantom script telling how rainbows are made and why they go away."

"Poetry is a section of river-fog and moving boat-lights, delivered between bridges and whistles, so one says, 'Oh!' and another, 'How?'"

"Poetry is a sequence of dots and dashes, spelling depths, crypts, cross-lights, and moon wisps."

INTRODUCTION

Few poets speak to everyone. Carl Sandburg does because he was a listener, a watcher, a lover of and spokesperson for all people. The voices of the people in his poems ring out: mothers, fathers, children, farmers, telephone operators, the rich and the poor—the poor rich and the rich poor. The things he wrote of speak, too: bubbles, birds, doors, grass, paper sacks, steel, fog, and the sea. Everyone, everything, has its moment.

His words are strong. They command attention: *Pile the bodies high at Austerlitz and Waterloo. . . . Look out how you use proud words. . . . Life is hard; be steel; be a rock.*

He poses probing questions: *When ice turns back into water does it remember it was ice? . . . When will man know what birds know?* And whimsical questions: *If you ask your mother for one fried egg for breakfast and she gives you two fried eggs and you eat both of them, who is better in arithmetic, you or your mother?*

He makes us think, see, feel, take notice.

Carl Sandburg's poetry is a world where children put beans in their ears, where a shirt is a signal and teller of souls, where there is poetry in neckties, where stars are so far away they never speak when spoken to.

My love affair with Carl Sandburg's work began some twenty-three years ago when I began teaching elementary school, sharing his poetry with children of all ages. It was then that I found his diverse body of verse, including the wonderfully delightful "Arithmetic," a selection I continue to use across the country, whether I am teaching 1+1 to first-graders, or marveling at the baffling principles of $E=MC^2$ with college-aged students or doctoral candidates.

His poems are ageless, filled with surprise; there is wonder in every line. He can be funny, serene, serious, sad.

The son of Swedish immigrants, Carl Sandburg was born on January 6, 1878, at 331 East Third Street in Galesburg, Illinois, a town located about 145 miles southwest of Chicago in Abraham Lincoln country. During his lifetime he worked as a laborer, secretary, newspaper reporter, political organizer, historian, lecturer, collector and singer of folksongs. He frequently toured the large urban cities of the United States and small, rural, out-of-the-way towns and villages with his guitar, singing folksongs and reciting his poems.

His first book of poetry, *Chicago Poems*, appeared in 1916, reflecting sturdy images—the tempo of everyday people's lives and language. His poetry, written in looping, free-verse style, was published at a rapid pace: *Cornhuskers* (1918), *Smoke and Steel* (1920), *Slabs of the Sunburnt West* (1922), *Good Morning, America* (1928), *The People, Yes* (1936), *Chicago Poems* (1950), *Harvest Poems 1910–1960* (1960), *Honey and Salt* (1963), and two collections for young readers, *Early Moon* (1930) and *Wind Song* (1960).

Thirty years of his life were devoted to preparing the monumental six-volume biography of Abraham Lincoln; in 1940, he received the Pulitzer Prize in History for the last four volumes, *Abraham Lincoln: The War Years.* In 1951, he was given a second Pulitzer Prize for *The Complete Poems.*

During his lifetime, Carl Sandburg wrote over eight hundred poems. *Rainbows Are Made* contains seventy verses selected from *The Complete Poems of Carl Sandburg, Revised and Expanded Edition* (1970). This new collection is divided into six sections dealing with sensitive views of people, word play at its best, observations of common, everyday things, nature notes, and his views of the sea and of night. Each section is introduced by one of the "Tentative (First Model) Definitions of Poetry," culled from the thirty-eight that precede his volume *Good Morning, America.*

Upon Carl Sandburg's death on July 22, 1967, at the age of eighty-nine, in Connemara, North Carolina, President Lyndon Baines Johnson issued this statement:

Carl Sandburg needs no epitaph. It is written for all time in the fields, the cities, the face and heart of the land he loved and the people he celebrated and inspired. With the world we mourn his passing. It is our pride and fortune as Americans that we will always hear Carl Sandburg's voice within ourselves. For he gave the truest and most enduring vision of our own greatness.

At the beginning of *Wind Song,* Carl Sandburg wrote:

> *Some poems may please you for*
> *half a minute & you don't care*
> *whether you keep them or not.*
> *Other poems you may feel to be*
> *priceless & you hug them to your*
> *heart and keep them for sure . . .*

May Carl Sandburg's words please each and every one of you. And do accept his wish: "May luck stars ever be over you."

Lee Bennett Hopkins
SCARBOROUGH, NEW YORK

RAINBOWS ARE MADE

"Poetry is a series of explanations of life, fading off into horizons too swift for explanations."

From

TIMESWEEP

There is only one horse on the earth
and his name is All Horses.
There is only one bird in the air
and his name is All Wings.
There is only one fish in the sea
and his name is All Fins.
There is only one man in the world
and his name is All Men.
There is only one woman in the world
and her name is All Women.
There is only one child in the world
and the child's name is All Children.
    There is only one Maker in the world
    and His children cover the earth
    and they are named All God's Children.

THE PEOPLE, YES

"I love you,"
said a great mother.
"I love you for what you are
knowing so well what you are.
And I love you more yet, child,
deeper yet than ever, child,
for what you are going to be,
knowing so well you are going far,
knowing your great works are ahead,
ahead and beyond,
yonder and far over yet."

From

THE PEOPLE, YES

A father sees a son nearing manhood.
What shall he tell that son?
"Life is hard; be steel; be a rock."
And this might stand him for the storms
and serve him for humdrum and monotony
and guide him amid sudden betrayals
and tighten him for slack moments.
"Life is a soft loam; be gentle; go easy."
And this too might serve him.
Brutes have been gentled where lashes failed.
The growth of a frail flower in a path up
has sometimes shattered and split a rock.
A tough will counts. So does desire.
So does a rich soft wanting.
Without rich wanting nothing arrives.

From

THE PEOPLE, YES

"Why did the children
put beans in their ears
when the one thing we told the children
they must not do
was put beans in their ears?"

"Why did the children
pour molasses on the cat
when the one thing we told the children
they must not do
was pour molasses on the cat?"

PHIZZOG

This face you got,
This here phizzog you carry around,
You never picked it out for yourself,
    at all, at all—did you?
This here phizzog—somebody handed it
    to you—am I right?
Somebody said, "Here's yours, now go see
    what you can do with it."
Somebody slipped it to you and it was like
    a package marked:
"No goods exchanged after being taken away"—
This face you got.

SOUP

I saw a famous man eating soup.
I say he was lifting a fat broth
Into his mouth with a spoon.
His name was in the newspapers that day
Spelled out in tall black headlines
And thousands of people were talking about him.

    When I saw him,
He sat bending his head over a plate
Putting soup in his mouth with a spoon.

MANUAL SYSTEM

Mary has a thingamajig clamped on her ears
And sits all day taking plugs out and sticking plugs in.
Flashes and flashes—voices and voices
                    calling for ears to pour words in
Faces at the ends of wires asking for other faces
                    at the ends of other wires:
All day taking plugs out and sticking plugs in,
Mary has a thingamajig clamped on her ears.

From

THE PEOPLE, YES

Phone girl: "I'm sorry I gave you the wrong number."
Man: "I'm sorry too, I know it was a perfectly good
number you gave me but I just couldn't use it."

CHOOSE

The single clenched fist lifted and ready,
Or the open asking hand held out and waiting.
              Choose:
For we meet by one or the other.

From

THE PEOPLE, YES

The white man drew a small circle in the sand
and told the red man, "This is what the Indian
knows," and drawing a big circle around the
small one, "This is what the white man knows."
The Indian took the stick and swept an immense
ring around both circles: "This is where the
white man and the red man know nothing."

From

THE PEOPLE, YES

The little girl saw her first troop parade and asked,
        "What are those?"
"Soldiers."
"What are soldiers?"
"They are for war. They fight and each tries to kill
        as many of the other side as he can."
The girl held still and studied.
"Do you know . . . I know something?"
"Yes, what is it you know?"
"Sometime they'll give a war and nobody will come."

GRASS

Pile the bodies high at Austerlitz and Waterloo.
Shovel them under and let me work—
                    I am the grass; I cover all.

And pile them high at Gettysburg
And pile them high at Ypres and Verdun.
Shovel them under and let me work.
Two years, ten years, and passengers ask the conductor:
                    What place is this?
                    Where are we now?

                    I am the grass.
                    Let me work.

COOL TOMBS

When Abraham Lincoln was shoveled into the tombs, he forgot the copperheads
and the assassin . . . in the dust, in the cool tombs.

And Ulysses Grant lost all thought of con men and Wall Street, cash and collateral
turned ashes . . . in the dust, in the cool tombs.

Pocahontas' body, lovely as a poplar, sweet as a red haw in November or a pawpaw
in May, did she wonder? does she remember? . . . in the dust, in the cool
tombs?

Take any streetful of people buying clothes and groceries, cheering a hero or throw-
ing confetti and blowing tin horns . . . tell me if the lovers are losers . . . tell me
if any get more than the lovers . . . in the dust . . . in the cool tombs.

From

THE PEOPLE, YES

Said the scorpion of hate: "The poor hate the rich. The rich hate the poor. The south hates the north. The west hates the east. The workers hate their bosses. The bosses hate their workers. The country hates the towns. The towns hate the country. We are a house divided against itself. We are millions of hands raised against each other. We are united in but one aim—getting the dollar. And when we get the dollar we employ it to get more dollars."

HUMDRUM

If I had a million lives to live
    and a million deaths to die
    in a million humdrum worlds,
I'd like to change my name
    and have a new house number to go by
    each and every time I died
    and started life all over again.

I wouldn't want the same name every time
    and the same old house number always,
    dying a million deaths,
    dying one by one a million times:
    —would you?
                    or you?
                            or you?

CADENZA

The knees
  of this proud woman
are bone.

The elbows
  of this proud woman
are bone.

The summer-white stars
  and the winter-white stars
never stop circling
  around this proud woman.

The bones
  of this proud woman
answer the vibrations
  of the stars.

  In summer
the stars speak deep thoughts
  In the winter
the stars repeat summer speeches.

The knees
  of this proud woman
know these thoughts
  and know these speeches
of the summer and winter stars.

SOUTHERN PACIFIC

Huntington sleeps in a house six feet long.
Huntington dreams of railroads he built and owned.
Huntington dreams of ten thousand men saying: Yes, sir.

Blithery sleeps in a house six feet long.
Blithery dreams of rails and ties he laid.
Blithery dreams of saying to Huntington: Yes, sir.

Huntington,
Blithery, sleep in houses six feet long.

ILLINOIS FARMER

Bury this old Illinois farmer with respect.
He slept the Illinois nights of his life after days of work in Illinois cornfields.
Now he goes on a long sleep.
The wind he listened to in the cornsilk and the tassels, the wind that
    combed his red beard zero mornings when the snow lay white on the
    yellow ears in the bushel basket at the corncrib,
The same wind will now blow over the place here where his hands must
    dream of Illinois corn.

"Poetry is a search for syllables to shoot at the barriers of the unknown and the unknowable."

IS WISDOM A LOT OF LANGUAGE?

Apes, may I speak to you a moment?
Chimpanzees, come hither for words.
Orangoutangs, let's get into a huddle.
Baboons, lemme whisper in your ears.
Gorillas, do yuh hear me hollerin' to yuh?
And monkeys! monkeys! get this chatter—

    For a long time men have plucked letters
    Out of the air and shaped syllables.
    And out of the syllables came words
    And from the words came phrases, clauses.
    Sentences were born—and languages.
    (The Tower of Babel didn't work out—
    it came down quicker than it went up.)
    Misunderstandings followed the languages,
    Arguments, epithets, maledictions, curses,
    Gossip, backbiting, the buzz of the bazoo,
    Chit chat, blah blah, talk just to be talking,
    Monologues of members telling other members
    How good they are now and were yesterday,
    Conversations missing the point,
    Dialogues seldom as beautiful as soliloquies,
    Seldom as fine as a man alone, a woman by herself
    Telling a clock, "I'm a plain damn fool."

Read the dictionary from A to Izzard today.
Get a vocabulary. Brush up on your diction.
See whether wisdom is just a lot of language.

LITTLE GIRL, BE CAREFUL WHAT YOU SAY

Little girl, be careful what you say
when you make talk with words, words—
for words are made of syllables
and syllables, child, are made of air—
and air is so thin—air is the breath of God—
air is finer than fire or mist,
finer than water or moonlight,
finer than spider-webs in the moon,
finer than water-flowers in the morning:
    and words are strong, too,
    stronger than rocks or steel
stronger than potatoes, corn, fish, cattle,
and soft, too, soft as little pigeon-eggs,
soft as the music of hummingbird wings.
    So, little girl, when you speak greetings,
when you tell jokes, make wishes or prayers,
    be careful, be careless, be careful,
    be what you wish to be.

PRIMER LESSON

Look out how you use proud words.
When you let proud words go, it is
    not easy to call them back.
They wear long boots, hard boots; they
    walk off proud; they can't hear you
    calling—
Look out how you use proud words.

BUBBLES

Two bubbles found they had rainbows on their curves.
They flickered out saying:
"It was worth being a bubble just to have held that
    rainbow thirty seconds."

BUFFALO DUSK

The buffaloes are gone.
And those who saw the buffaloes are gone.
Those who saw the buffaloes by thousands and how they pawed the
    prairie sod into dust with their hoofs, their great heads down pawing
    on in a great pageant of dusk,
Those who saw the buffaloes are gone.
And the buffaloes are gone.

METAMORPHOSIS

    When water turns ice does it remember
one time it was water?
    When ice turns back into water does it
remember it was ice?

BUNDLES

I have thought of beaches, fields,
Tears, laughter.

I have thought of homes put up—
And blown away.

I have thought of meetings and for
Every meeting a good-by.

I have thought of stars going alone,
Orioles in pairs, sunsets in blundering
Wistful deaths.

I have wanted to let go and cross over
To a next star, a last star.

I have asked to be left a few tears
And some laughter.

BIRD TALK

And now when the branches were beginning to be heavy,
It was the time when they once had said, "This is the
    beginning of summer."
The shrilling of the frogs was not so shrill as in the
    first weeks after the broken winter;
The birds took their hops and zigzags a little more
    anxious; a home is a home; worms are worms.
The yellow spreads of the dandelions and buttercups
    reached across the green pastures.
Tee whee and *tee whee* came on the breezes, and the grackles
    chuzzled their syllables.
And it was the leaves with a strong soft wind over them
    that talked most of all and said more than any others
    though speaking the fewest words.
It was the green leaves trickling out the gaunt nowhere
    of winter, out on the gray hungry branches—
It was the leaves on the branches, beginning to be heavy,
    who said as they said one time before, "This is the be-
    ginning of summer."

We shall never blame the birds who come
    where the river and the road make the Grand Crossing
    and talk there, sitting in circles talking bird talk.
If they ask in their circles as to who is here
    and as to who is not here and who used to be here,
Or if instead of counting up last year as against
    this year, they count up this year as against next
    year, and have their bird chatter about who is here
    this year who won't be here next year,
We shall never blame the birds.

If I have put your face among leaf faces, child,
Or if I have put your voice among bird voices,
Blame me no more than the bluejays.

WINGTIP

The birds—are they worth remembering?
Is flight a wonder and one wingtip a
space marvel?
When will man know what birds know?

From

HEAVY AND LIGHT

Fritters used to say, "There is poetry in neckties."
He picked neckties with a theory of color and design.
He knew haberdashers the way book bugs know where second-hand book-
    stores are.
For a picnic he wore pink, for a fall fog day a gray blue,
And a four-in-hand, a bow, a bat-eye, each in its separate individual silk,
    plain or striped or spotted,
Each had its message, its poem, its reminders, for Fritters.
"I know how to pick 'em," he used to say, "I know the right scarf for
    either a wedding or a funeral or a poker party, there is poetry in
    neckties."

DIFFERENT KINDS OF GOOD-BY

Good-by is a loose word, a yellow ribbon
    fluttering in the wind.
Good-by is a stiff word, a steel slide rule—
    a fixed automatic phone number.
A thousand people? And you must say good-by
    to all? One at a time?—yes, I guess you
    need a thousand different good-bys.
There is a good-by for the Johnsons and another
    for the Smiths and another for the Poindexters
    and the Van Rensselaers.
And there is the big grand good-by to the thousand
    all at once, the whole works.

"Poetry is a shuffling of boxes of illusions buckled with a strap of facts."

From

SKETCH OF A POET

He wastes time walking and telling the air, "I am superior even to the wind."

On several proud days he has addressed the wide circumambient atmosphere, "I am the wind myself."

He has poet's license 4-11-44; he got it even before writing of those "silver bugs that come on the sky without warning every evening."

He stops for the buzzing of bumblebees on bright Tuesdays in any summer month; he performs with a pencil all alone among dun cattails, amid climbing juniper bushes, notations rivaling the foot tracks of anxious spiders; he finds mice homes under beach logs in the sand and pursues inquiries on how the mice have one room for bed-room, dining-room, sitting-room and how they have no front porch where they sit publicly and watch passers-by.

DOORS

An open door says, "Come in."
A shut door says, "Who are you?"
Shadows and ghosts go through shut doors.
If a door is shut and you want it shut,
    why open it?
If a door is open and you want it open,
    why shut it?
Doors forget but only doors know what it is
    doors forget.

BOXES AND BAGS

The bigger the box the more it holds.
Empty boxes hold the same as empty heads.
Enough small empty boxes thrown into a big empty box fill it full.
A half-empty box says, "Put more in."
A big enough box could hold the world.
Elephants need big boxes to hold a dozen elephant handkerchiefs.
Fleas fold little handkerchiefs and fix them nice and neat in flea
    handkerchief-boxes.
Bags lean against each other and boxes stand independent.
Boxes are square with corners unless round with circles.
Box can be piled on box till the whole works comes tumbling.
Pile box on box and the bottom box says, "If you will kindly take notice
    you will see it all rests on me."
Pile box on box and the top one says, "Who falls farthest if or when we
    fall? I ask you."
Box people go looking for boxes and bag people go looking for bags.

PAPER I

Paper is two kinds, to write on, to wrap with.
If you like to write, you write.
If you like to wrap, you wrap.
Some papers like writers, some like wrappers.
Are you a writer or a wrapper?

PAPER II

I write what I know on one side of the paper
    and what I don't know on the other.
Fire likes dry paper and wet paper laughs at
    fire.
Empty paper sacks say, "Put something in me,
    what are we waiting for?"
Paper sacks packed to the limit say, "We hope
    we don't bust."
Paper people like to meet other paper people.

From

PENCILS

Pencils
telling where the wind comes from
    open a story.

Pencils
telling where the wind goes
    end a story.

These eager pencils
come to a stop
. . . only . . . when the stars high over
come to a stop.

ARITHMETIC

Arithmetic is where numbers fly like pigeons in and out of your head.

Arithmetic tells you how many you lose or win if you know how many you had before you lost or won.

Arithmetic is seven eleven all good children go to heaven—or five six bundle of sticks.

Arithmetic is numbers you squeeze from your head to your hand to your pencil to your paper till you get the answer.

Arithmetic is where the answer is right and everything is nice and you can look out of the window and see the blue sky—or the answer is wrong and you have to start all over and try again and see how it comes out this time.

If you take a number and double it and double it again and then double it a few more times, the number gets bigger and bigger and goes higher and higher and only arithmetic can tell you what the number is when you decide to quit doubling.

Arithmetic is where you have to multiply—and you carry the multiplication table in your head and hope you won't lose it.

If you have two animal crackers, one good and one bad, and you eat one and a striped zebra with streaks all over him eats the other, how many animal crackers will you have if somebody offers you five six seven and you say No no no and you say Nay nay nay and you say Nix nix nix?

If you ask your mother for one fried egg for breakfast and she gives you two fried eggs and you eat both of them, who is better in arithmetic, you or your mother?

From

THE PEOPLE, YES

Money is power: so said one.
Money is a cushion: so said another.
Money is the root of evil: so said
    still another.
Money means freedom: so runs an old
    saying.

And money is all of these—and more.
Money pays for whatever you want—if
    you have the money.
Money buys food, clothes, houses, land,
    guns, jewels, men, women, time to be
    lazy and listen to music.
Money buys everything except love,
    personality, freedom, immortality,
    silence, peace.

SHIRT

My shirt is a token and symbol,
more than a cover for sun and rain,
my shirt is a signal,
and a teller of souls.

I can take off my shirt and tear it,
and so make a ripping razzly noise,
and the people will say,
"Look at him tear his shirt."

I can keep my shirt on.
I can stick around and sing like a little bird
and look 'em all in the eye and never be fazed.
    I can keep my shirt on.

THE HAMMER

I have seen
The old gods go
And the new gods come.

Day by day
And year by year
The idols fall
And the idols rise.

Today
I worship the hammer.

PRAYERS OF STEEL

Lay me on an anvil, O God.
Beat me and hammer me into a crowbar.
Let me pry loose old walls.
Let me lift and loosen old foundations.

Lay me on an anvil, O God.
Beat me and hammer me into a steel spike.
Drive me into the girders that hold a skyscraper together.
Take red-hot rivets and fasten me into the central girders.
Let me be the great nail holding a skyscraper through blue nights into
    white stars.

WAS EVER A DREAM A DRUM?

Was ever a dream a drum
  or a drum a dream?
Can a drummer drum a dream
  or a dreamer dream a drum?
The drum in a dream
  pounds loud to the dreamer.

Now the moon tonight over Indiana
is a fire-drum of a phantom dreamer.

"Poetry is a phantom script telling how rainbows are made and why they go away."

ELM BUDS

Elm buds are out.
Yesterday morning, last night,
   they crept out.
They are the mice of early
   spring air.

To the north is the gray sky.
Winter hung it gray for the gray
   elm to stand dark against.
Now the branches all end with the
   yellow and gold mice of early
   spring air.
They are moving mice creeping out
   with leaf and leaf.

From

SANTA FE SKETCHES

In April the little farmers go out in the foothills,
up the mountain patches.
They go to gamble against the weather, the rain.

"If the rain comes like last year, we shall have a fat
winter,
If the rain comes like year before last, it is a lean
Christmas for us."

They put in their beans, the magic frijole, the chile,
they stretch open hands to the sky,
and tell the rain to come,
to come, come, come.

With a willing rain the gamblers win.
If the rain says, "Not this year," they lose.

So the little farmers go out in the foothills,
up the mountain patches in April,
telling every bean in the sack
to send up a wish to God
for water to come . . . out of the sky.

SPRING CRIES

1

Call us back, call us with your sliding silver,
Frogs of the early spring, frogs of the later days
When spring crosses over, when spring spills over
And spills the last of its sliding silvers
Into the running wind, the running water, of summer.
Call us back then, call over, call under—only call—
Frogs of the early spring, frogs of the later days.

2

Birds we have seen and known and counted,
Birds we have never learned the names of,
Call us back, you too, call us back.
Out of the forks and angles of branches,
High out of the blacksmith arms of oak and ash,
Sweet out of the Lombardy poplar's arrow head,
Soft out of the swinging, swaying,
The bending and almost broken branch
Of the bush of the home of the wild gooseberry—
Yellow feather, white throat, gray neck, red wing,
Scarlet head, blue shoulder, copper silver body line—
All you birds—call us back—call us under, over—
Birds we know, birds we never can know,
Birds spilling your one-two-three
Of a slur and a cry and a trill—
Call us back, you too call us.

3

Warble us easy and old ones.
Open your gates up the sunset in the evening.
Lift up your windows of song in the morning lights.
Wind on your spiral and zigzag ways.
Birds, we have heard baskets of you, bushes of you.
In a tree of a hundred windows ten of you sat
On the song sills of every window.
Warble us easy and old ones now.
Call us back, spill your one-two-three
Of a slur and a cry and a trill.

From

LINES WRITTEN FOR GENE KELLY TO DANCE TO

Spring is when the grass turns green and glad.
Spring is when the new grass comes up and says, "Hey, hey!
  Hey, hey!"
Be dizzy now and turn your head upside down and see how
  the world looks upside down.
Be dizzy now and turn a cartwheel, and see the good earth
  through a cartwheel.

Tell your feet the alphabet.
Tell your feet the multiplication table.
Tell your feet where to go, and watch 'em go and come back.

Can you dance a question mark?
Can you dance an exclamation point?
Can you dance a couple of commas?
And bring it to a finish with a period?

Can you dance like the wind is pushing you?
Can you dance like you are pushing the wind?
Can you dance with slow wooden heels
  and then change to bright and singing silver heels?
Such nice feet, such good feet.

CORN AND BEANS

Having looked long at two garden rows
And seen how the rain and dirt have used them
I have decided the corn and beans shall have names.

And one is to be known as the Thwarted Corn of a Short Year
While the other shall be called the Triumphant Beans of Plenty Rain.

If I change these names next Sunday I shall let you know about it.

From

CROSSING OHIO WHEN POPPIES BLOOM IN ASHTABULA

Pick me poppies in Ohio,
mother.
Pick me poppies in a back yard
in Ashtabula.
May going, poppies coming, summer humming:
make it a poppy summer, mother; the leaves
sing in the silk, the leaves sing a tawny
red gold; seven sunsets saved themselves
to be here now.

Pick me poppies, mother; go, May; wash me,
summer; shoot up this back yard in Ashtabula, shoot it up, give us a daylight fireworks in Ohio, burn it up with tawny red
gold.

FOURTH OF JULY NIGHT

The little boat at anchor
in black water sat murmuring
to the tall black sky.

. . .

A white sky bomb fizzed on a black line.
A rocket hissed its red signature into the west.
Now a shower of Chinese fire alphabets,
a cry of flower pots broken in flames,
a long curve to a purple spray,
three violet balloons—
    Drips of seaweed tangled in gold,
    shimmering symbols of mixed numbers,
    tremulous arrangements of cream gold folds
    of a bride's wedding gown—

. . .

A few sky bombs spoke their pieces,
then velvet dark.

The little boat at anchor
in black water sat murmuring
to the tall black sky.

NOCTURN CABBAGE

Cabbages catch at the moon.
It is late summer, no rain, the pack of the soil
    cracks open, it is a hard summer.

In the night the cabbages catch at the moon, the
    leaves drip silver, the rows of cabbages are
    series of little silver waterfalls in the moon.

HARVEST

When the corn stands yellow in September,
A red flower ripens and shines among the stalks
And a red silk creeps among the broad ears
And tall tassels lift over all else
                and keep a singing
                to the prairies
                and the wind.

        They are the grand lone ones
        For they are never saved
            along with the corn:

          They are cut down
          and piled high
          and burned.

          Their fire
          lights the west in November.

PROUD TORSOS

Just before the high time of autumn
Comes with the crush of its touch,
And the leaves fall, the leaves one by one,
The leaves by a full darkening sky fall,
The trees look proud, the horse chestnut
Stands with a gathered pride, the ivies
Are gathered around the stumps,
The ivies are woven thick with a green coat
Covering the stumps. Yes, the trees
Look proud now, it is the big time.
Have they not all had summer?
Didn't they all flimmer with faint
Lines of green in the spring,
A thin green mist as if it might
Be air or it might be new green leaves?
So, the first weeks of September are on
And each tree stands with a murmur,
"I stand here with a count of one more year,
One more number, one more ring in my torso."
Two weeks, five, six weeks, and the trees
Will be standing . . . stripped . . . gaunt . . .
The leaves gone . . . the coat of green gone . . .
And they will be proud but no longer
With the gathered pride of the days
In the high time.

CRABAPPLES

Sweeten these bitter wild crabapples, Illinois
October sun. The roots here came from the
wilderness, came before man came here. They
are bitter as the wild is bitter.

Give these crabapples your softening gold,
October sun, go through to the white wet
seeds inside and soften them black. Make
these bitter apples sweet. They want you, sun.

The drop and the fall, the drop and the fall,
the apples leaving the branches for the black
earth under, they know you from last year,
the year before last year, October sun.

SPLINTER

The voice of the last cricket
across the first frost
is one kind of good-by.
It is so thin a splinter of singing.

"Poetry is a section of river-fog and moving boat-lights, delivered between bridges and whistles, so one says, 'Oh!' and another, 'How?'"

SEA CHEST

There was a woman loved a man
as the man loved the sea.
Her thoughts of him were the same
as his thoughts of the sea.
They made an old sea chest for their belongings
together.

From

NORTH ATLANTIC

The sea is always the same:
and yet the sea always changes.

    The sea gives all,
    and yet the sea keeps something back.

The sea takes without asking.
The sea is a worker, a thief and a loafer.
    Why does the sea let go so slow?
    Or never let go at all?

The sea always the same
day after day,
the sea always the same
night after night,
fog on fog and never a star,
wind on wind and running white sheets,
bird on bird always a sea-bird—
so the days get lost:
it is neither Saturday nor Monday,
it is any day or no day,
it is a year, ten years.

YOUNG SEA

The sea is never still.
It pounds on the shore
Restless as a young heart,
Hunting.

The sea speaks
And only the stormy hearts
Know what it says:
It is the face
          of a rough mother speaking.

The sea is young.
One storm cleans all the hoar
And loosens the age of it.
I hear it laughing, reckless.

They love the sea,
Men who ride on it
And know they will die
Under the salt of it.

Let only the young come,
    Says the sea.
Let them kiss my face
    And hear me.
I am the last word
    And I tell
Where storms and stars come from.

OLD DEEP SING-SONG

in the old deep sing-song of the sea
in the old going-on of that sing-song
in that old mama-mama-mama going-on
of that nightlong daylong sleepsong
we look on   we listen
we lay by and hear
too many big bells   too many long gongs
too many weepers over a lost gone gold
too many laughs over light green gold
woven and changing in the wash and the heave
moving on the bottoms   winding in the waters
sending themselves with arms and voices
up in the old mama-mama-mama music
up into the whirl of spokes of light

SEA SLANT

On up the sea slant,
On up the horizon,
This ship limps.

The bone of her nose fog-gray,
The heart of her sea-strong,
She came a long way,
She goes a long way.

On up the horizon,
On up the sea-slant,
She limps sea-strong, fog-gray.

She is a green-lit night gray.
She comes and goes in sea fog.
Up the horizon slant she limps.

SKETCH

The shadows of the ships
Rock on the crest
In the low blue lustre
Of the tardy and the soft inrolling tide.

A long brown bar at the dip of the sky
Puts an arm of sand in the span of salt.

The lucid and endless wrinkles
Draw in, lapse and withdraw.
Wavelets crumble and white spent bubbles
Wash on the floor of the beach.

    Rocking on the crest
    In the low blue lustre
    Are the shadows of the ships.

LOST

Desolate and lone
All night long on the lake
Where fog trails and mist creeps,
The whistle of a boat
Calls and cries unendingly,
Like some lost child
In tears and trouble
Hunting the harbor's breast
And the harbor's eyes.

RIVER MOONS

The double moon, one on the high backdrop of the west, one on the
    curve of the river face,
The sky moon of fire and the river moon of water, I am taking these
    home in a basket, hung on an elbow, such a teeny weeny elbow, in
    my head.
I saw them last night, a cradle moon, two horns of a moon, such an early
    hopeful moon, such a child's moon for all young hearts to make a
    picture of.
The river—I remember this like a picture—the river was the upper twist
    of a written question mark.
I know now it takes many many years to write a river, a twist of water
    asking a question.
And white stars moved when the moon moved, and one red star kept burning,
    and the Big Dipper was almost overhead.

"Poetry is a sequence of dots and dashes, spelling depths, crypts, cross-lights, and moon wisps."

FOG

The fog comes
on little cat feet.

It sits looking
over harbor and city
on silent haunches
and then moves on.

WINDOW

Night from a railroad car window
Is a great, dark, soft thing
Broken across with slashes of light.

BRIGHT CONVERSATION WITH SAINT-EX

When the smoke of the clouds parted
there came on the night blue of sky
the brighter blue of a little star
tremulous with hazards of travel.
And why should I have been saying,
    "Go forth, little star.
    Be not afraid, small traveller.
    Remember it holds importance
    for you to be what you are
    and be seen where you are
    by random gazers like me"?
And I am asking why I should tell a star
    to go on being a star.

From

THE PEOPLE, YES

In the long flat panhandle of Texas
far off on the grassland of the cattle country
near noon they sight a rider coming toward them
and the sky may be a cold neverchanging gray
or the sky may be changing its numbers
back and forth all day even and odd numbers
and the afternoon slides away somewhere
and they see their rider is alive yet
their rider is coming nearer yet
and they expect what happens and it happens again
he and his horse ride in late for supper
yet not too late
and night is on and the stars are out
and night too slides away somewhere
night too has even and odd numbers.

The wind brings "a norther"
to the long flat panhandle
and in the shivering cold they say:
        "Between Amarilla and the North Pole
        is only a barbwire fence,"
which they give a twist:
        "Out here the only windbreak
        is the North Star."

STARS

The stars are too many to count.
The stars make sixes and sevens.
The stars tell nothing—and everything.
The stars look scattered.
Stars are so far away they never speak
    when spoken to.

From
TWO MOON FANTASIES

The moon is a bucket of suds
yellow and smooth suds.
The horses of the moon dip their heads
into this bucket and drink.
The cats of the moon, the dogs, the rats,
they too go to this bucket for drink.
Thus an apparition told it.
To him the moon meant drink and drinkers.

The moon is a disc of hidden books.
Reach an arm into it
and feel around with your hands
and you bring out books already written
and many books yet to be written
for the moon holds past, present, future.
Thus an apparition related the matter.
To him the disc meant print and printers.

AUCTIONEER

Now I go down here and bring up a moon.
How much am I bid for the moon?
You see it a bright moon and brand-new.
What can I get to start it?   how much?
What! who ever ever heard such a bid for a moon?
   Come now, gentlemen, come.
This is a solid guaranteed moon.
You may never have another chance
   to make a bid on such a compact
   eighteen-carat durable gold moon.
You could shape a thousand wedding rings
   out of this moongold.
I can guarantee the gold and the weddings
   will last forever
   and then a thousand years more.
Come gentlemen, no nonsense, make me a bid.

MOON RONDEAU

"Love is a door we shall open together."
So they told each other under the moon
One evening when the smell of leaf mould
And the beginnings of roses and potatoes
Came on a wind.

Late in the hours of that evening
They looked long at the moon and called it
A silver button, a copper coin, a bronze wafer,
A plaque of gold, a vanished diadem,
A brass hat dripping from deep waters.

      "People like us,
          us two,
      We own the moon."

GOOD NIGHT

Many ways to spell good night.

Fireworks at a pier on the Fourth of July
    spell it with red wheels and yellow spokes.
They fizz in the air, touch the water and quit.
Rockets make a trajectory of gold-and-blue
    and then go out.

Railroad trains at night spell with a smokestack mushrooming a white
    pillar.

Steamboats turn a curve in the Mississippi crying in a baritone that crosses
    lowland cottonfields to a razorback hill.

It is easy to spell good night.
                    Many ways to spell good night.

INDEX OF TITLES

INDEX OF FIRST LINES

Many ways to spell good night.   77
Mary has a thingamajig clamped on her ears   10
Money is power: so said one.   41
My shirt is a token and symbol,   42

Night from a railroad car window   71
Now I go down here and bring up a moon.   75

On up the sea slant,   65

Paper is two kinds, to write on, to wrap with.   38
Pencils   39
Phone girl: "I'm sorry I gave you the wrong number."   10
Pick me poppies in Ohio,   53
Pile the bodies high at Austerlitz and Waterloo.   13

Said the scorpion of hate: "The poor hate the rich. The rich hate the poor. The
   south   15
Spring is when the grass turns green and glad.   52
Sweeten these bitter wild crabapples, Illinois   57

The bigger the box the more it holds.   37
The birds—are they worth remembering?   29
The buffaloes are gone.   26
The double moon, one on the high backdrop of the west, one on the   67
The fog comes   71
The knees   17
The little boat at anchor   54
The little girl saw her first troop parade and asked,   12
The moon is a bucket of suds   74
The sea is always the same: 62
The sea is never still.   63
The shadows of the ships   66
The single clenched fist lifted and ready,   11
The stars are too many to count.   74
The voice of the last cricket   57
The white man drew a small circle in the sand   11
There is only one horse on the earth   5
There was a woman loved a man   61